NBA CHAMPIONSHIP:

↓

1958

↓

ALL-TIME LEADING SCORER:

↓

DOMINIQUE WILKINS (1982–94):

↓

23,292 POINTS

THE NBA: A HISTORY OF HOOPS

ATLANTA HAWKS

BY JIM WHITING

CREATIVE EDUCATION   CREATIVE PAPERBACKS

Published by Creative Education
and Creative Paperbacks

P.O. Box 227, Mankato, Minnesota 56002

Creative Education and Creative Paperbacks
are imprints of The Creative Company

www.thecreativecompany.us

Design and production by Blue Design
Printed in the United States of America

Photographs by Alamy (David Dobbs), AP Images
(ASSOCIATED PRESS), Corbis (Corbis, Steve
Lipovsky, Toby Massey/AP, Andrew Snook/Icon
SMI), Getty Images (Bettmann, John Biever/Sports
Illustrated, Nathaniel S. Butler/NBAE, Kevin C.
Cox, Scott Cunningham/NBAE, Gary G. Dineen/
Sporting News, Focus on Sport, Jesse D. Garrabrant
/NBAE, Noah Graham/NBAE, Phil Huber/Sports
Illustrated, George Long/Wireimage, John W.
McDonough/Sports Illustrated, Richard Meek/
Sports Illustrated, Maddie Meyer/Getty Images
Sport, Jason Miller, Doug Pensinger/Getty Images
Sport, Damian Strohmeyer/Sports Illustrated),
Newscom (Mark Halmas/Icon SMI 483)

Library of Congress Cataloging-in-Publication Data

Names: Whiting, Jim, 1943- author.

Title: Atlanta Hawks / Jim Whiting.

Series: The NBA: A History of Hoops.

Includes bibliographical references and index.

Summary: This high-interest title summarizes
the history of the Atlanta Hawks professional
basketball team, highlighting memorable events
and noteworthy players such as Dominique Wilkins.

Identifiers: LCCN 2016046220 / ISBN 978-1-
60818-835-2 (hardcover) / ISBN 978-1-62832-438-9
(pbk) / ISBN 978-1-56660-883-1 (eBook)

Subjects: LCSH: 1. Atlanta Hawks (Basketball
team)—History—Juvenile literature.
2. Atlanta Hawks (Basketball team)—
Biography—Juvenile literature.

Classification: LCC GV885.52.A7 W547 2017 /
DDC 796.323/6409758231—dc23

CCSS: RI.4.1, 2, 3, 4; RI.5.1, 2, 4; RI.6.1, 2,
3; RF.4.3, 4; RF.5.3, 4; RH. 6-8. 4, 5, 7

First Edition HC 9 8 7 6 5 4 3 2 1
First Edition PBK 9 8 7 6 5 4 3 2 1

CONTENTS

LEGENDS OF THE HARDWOOD

8

At 630 feet (192 m), the Gateway Arch in **ST. LOUIS** is the nation's tallest monument.

MEET ME IN ST. LOUIS

Hawks supporters slumped in their seats. It was Game 6 of the 1958 National Basketball Association (NBA) Finals. The defending champion Boston Celtics led by two into the final

Forward **BOB PETTIT** led the Hawks in scoring for more than a decade.

quarter. If they won, the deciding Game 7 would be in Boston. Burly Hawks forward Bob Pettit didn't want that to happen. He pushed through his guards. He drained shot after shot. With 16 seconds left, the Hawks clung to a one-point lead. A teammate missed a shot. Pettit muscled his way past a horde of Celtics. He tipped in the field goal that made the Hawks world champions! Pettit had scored an amazing 50 points, including 19 of his team's final 21. It was a new playoff scoring record.

10

At that time, the Hawks played their games in St. Louis, Missouri. Twelve years before that, they were in the Tri-Cities area. (Three neighboring towns in Iowa and Illinois are known as the Tri-Cities.) As the Tri-Cities Blackhawks, the team belonged to the National Basketball League (NBL). In 1949, they advanced to the league championship semifinals before losing. The star player was 6-foot-10 center Don Otten.

WIN ... OR ELSE

The Blackhawks began the 1950–51 season with Dave McMillan as head coach. When the team struggled to a 9–14 record, owner Ben Kerner fired McMillan. Guard John Logan became player/coach. He lasted only three games (two wins). Forward/center Mike Todorovich finished the season with a 14–28 mark. The team's 25–43 record placed it last in the NBA Western Division. Kerner's impatience showed again in 1961–62. He fired coach Paul Seymour after a 5–9 start. Seymour's replacement, Andrew "Fuzzy" Levane, lost 40 of the next 60 games. Pettit guided the team to a 4–2 mark to end the season. The Hawks' 29–51 record nearly dropped them into the cellar.

Later that year, the NBL merged with the Basketball Association of America (BAA). The new league became the NBA. The Blackhawks didn't play well at first. Fan support decreased. Owner Ben Kerner moved the team to Milwaukee after the 1950–51 season. He also renamed the team the Hawks. The team continued its losing ways. In 1954, the Hawks drafted Pettit. He was voted Rookie of the Year. But the team still finished last in the NBA's Western Division.

Kerner moved the team to St. Louis for the 1955–56 season. The Hawks were an instant hit in their new home. They advanced to the Western Division finals. The following year, they played for the NBA championship. They lost to Boston, four games to three. That set the stage for the Hawks' 1958 championship. Years later, Pettit clearly remembered that victory. "It was a great feeling," he said. "It was the

Guard **LENNY WILKENS** was a reliable playmaker for the Hawks.

highlight of my 11-year professional career, no doubt. It's something you look back on forever."

Everyone looked forward to a possible rematch the following season. The Hawks compiled a 49–23 record. But they lost in the Western Division finals. Buoyed by the addition of players such as crafty guard Lenny Wilkens and muscular center Clyde Lovellette, the Hawks returned to the title series in 1960 and 1961. They lost both times to the Celtics. After losing 51 games in 1961–62, the Hawks clawed their way back. Between 1963 and 1967, they played for the Western Division championship four times. Three of those four times, they dropped the last game of a seven-game series. They won a franchise-best 56 games in the following season.

FLYING TO ATLANTA

n 1968, Kerner sold the team to a group of Atlanta businessmen. The Hawks' first two seasons in their new nest continued to be successful. Newcomers such as high-scoring guard Lou Hudson helped the team

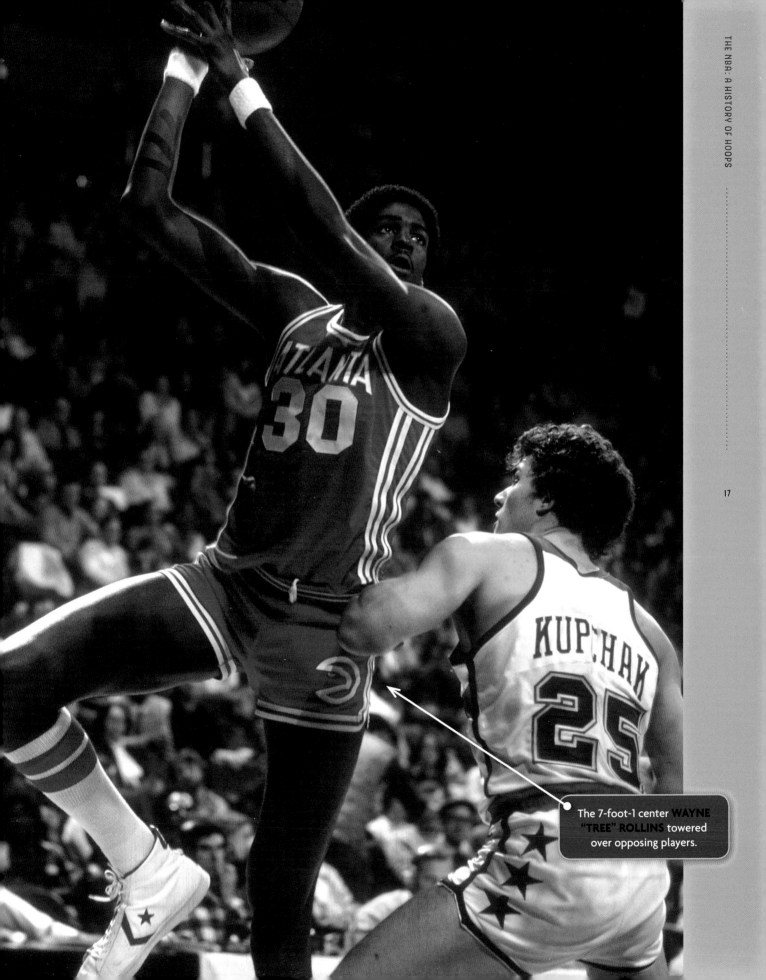

The 7-foot-1 center **WAYNE "TREE" ROLLINS** towered over opposing players.

Guard **JOE CALDWELL** was known as "Pogo Joe" for his leaping ability.

reach the playoffs. Both times, they again fell just short of playing for the NBA championship. A realignment of the NBA for the 1970–71 season put Atlanta in the Eastern Conference.

Atlanta added flashy guard "Pistol Pete" Maravich that same season. His floppy long hair and ability to score from seemingly impossible angles made him an instant fan favorite. With the pistol firing steadily, the Hawks made the playoffs for three more years in a row. Each time,

LEGENDS OF THE HARDWOOD

HARD WORK PAYS OFF

BOB PETTIT, CENTER/POWER FORWARD, 6-FOOT-9, 1954–65

Bob Pettit was cut from his high school freshman basketball team in Baton Rouge, Louisiana. The same thing happened the next year. He was barely good enough to play in a church league. "Don't give up," his father told him. "Keep practicing." Bob practiced every day after school. As a junior, he was named to the All-City team. He became a star in college. But some people thought he was too slow and not big enough to play professional basketball. Bob proved them wrong. "He kept coming at you more than any man in the game. He was always battling for position, fighting you off the boards," said legendary Boston Celtics center Bill Russell. Pettit scored more than 20,000 points in his career.

Atlanta reached the playoffs 18 times under **TED TURNER'S** ownership.

though, they were eliminated in the conference semifinals. But then the team began drifting downward in the standings. It had four straight losing seasons and didn't qualify for the playoffs. Atlanta traded Maravich. Fan support dropped.

Rumors flew that the team might be sold and moved from Atlanta. Ted Turner bought the team in 1977. He was a wealthy Atlanta media businessman who also owned the Atlanta Braves baseball team. He guaranteed the Hawks would stay in Atlanta. "He is one of the most colorful owners we've ever had," NBA commissioner David Stern said later of Turner. "No one has been as loyal and as committed as he was, and I am proud to be associated with him."

With their financial situation secure, the Hawks began moving upward again. One key was the addition of shot-blocking center and

"SWEET" LOU HUDSON had one of the smoothest jump shots in the NBA.

22

rebounder Wayne "Tree" Rollins. "Tree is the type of guy you hope to

have around for 10 years," noted Hawks coach Hubie Brown. "He has

a great work ethic and gives you everything he has every night." The

team returned to the playoffs with a 41–41 record in 1977–78, Rollins'

first year. The Hawks notched even better records the following two

seasons. But all three times they made early exits from the playoffs.

Team officials knew they needed a big scoring threat. They hadn't had

one after trading Hudson in 1977.

STATUESQUE

DOMINIQUE WILKINS, SMALL FORWARD, 6-FOOT-8, 1982–94

To honor Dominique Wilkins and his contributions, the Hawks unveiled a statue of the legend in March 2015 outside Philips Arena. It is 13.5 feet (4.1 m) tall. The statue is made of bronze and stands atop a granite base. It captures Wilkins in a classic pose—just before launching one of his dunks. "What bigger stage to stand on than to have a statue of you in front of the franchise and building that you love?" Wilkins said. "I know nobody who loves this organization like I do … I bleed and breathe Hawks. Even when I played for other teams, I felt funny."

24

THE HUMAN HIGHLIGHT FILM

The Hawks finally found that scoring threat in 1982. They chose forward Dominique Wilkins in the NBA Draft. Wilkins became known as the "Human Highlight Film." He made spectacular soaring dunks.

Forward **DOMINIQUE WILKINS** thrilled fans with his highflying style of play.

"YOU CAN MAKE BAD TRADES, YOU CAN MAKE TRADES THAT SET A FRANCHISE BACK A FEW YEARS, OR YOU CAN MAKE MOVES THAT COMPLETELY RUIN A SPORT IN A CITY."

With the aid of players such as guard Glenn "Doc" Rivers, Atlanta posted an all-time best record of 57–25. But it was bounced in the first round of the playoffs. After a 34–48 record in 1984–85, Atlanta roared back to go 50–32. Wilkins won the NBA scoring title with an average of 30.3 points per game. But Atlanta lost in the Eastern Conference semifinals.

The Hawks recorded another 57–25 mark in 1986–87. Atlanta fans dreamed of the team's second-ever NBA title. But that dream turned into a nightmare when the team lost to the Detroit Pistons in the conference semifinals. The Hawks won just one of five games. With a 50–32 record in 1987–88, the team had its third straight winning season. But once again, it lost in the conference semifinals. This time, Boston was the opponent. The final game featured an epic fourth-quarter scoring duel between Wilkins and Celtics legend Larry Bird. The team had its fourth straight 50-victory season in 1988–89, which ended with a quick exit in the playoffs.

A series of crippling injuries dropped the team out of the playoffs the following year. The three seasons after that showed little improvement. Wilkins still played at a high level. He surpassed Pettit as the Hawks' all-time leading scorer in the 1992–93 season. Then things improved dramatically. Lenny Wilkens returned to the team as head coach. He emphasized defense, symbolized by guard Mookie Blaylock's 2.62 steals per game. Wilkens was named Coach of the Year. But his magic ran out

DANNY MANNING averaged 18 points a game against Miami in the 1994 playoffs.

in the conference semifinals. The heavily favored Hawks lost to Indiana, four games to two.

For many people, the season's success was overshadowed by the midseason trade of Dominique Wilkins. It is the only time in NBA history that a team in first place traded its leading scorer following the All-Star break. "That trade ruined pro basketball in Atlanta," noted *Sports Illustrated* writer Lang Whitaker. "You can make bad trades, you can make trades that set a franchise back a few years, or you can make moves that completely ruin a sport in a city. Atlanta lost their only NBA hero."

29

PISTOL PETE

PETE MARAVICH, GUARD, 6-FOOT-5, 1970–74

Pete Maravich's ability to shoot a basketball led to his nickname of "Pistol Pete." He set college basketball records of 3,667 career points and averaged 44.2 points. He averaged 24 points a game with Atlanta. He was especially noted for his behind-the-back dribbling and seeing-eye passes to teammates. Not everyone approved of his wide-open playing style. "His playground moves, circus shots, and hotdog passes were considered outrageous during his era," notes the *NBA Encyclopedia*. Sadly, Pistol Pete died from a heart attack in a pickup game in 1988. Eight years later, a panel of NBA coaches and players named him one of the 50 greatest NBA players. "The best ball-handler of all time was Pete Maravich," said Boston Hall of Famer John Havlicek.

Intimidating center DIKEMBE MUTOMBO grabbed rebounds under the basket.

FROM WINNERS TO WASHOUTS

ven without Wilkins, the team returned to the playoffs for the next five years. The Hawks compiled winning records each time. One factor was the addition of center Dikembe Mutombo in 1996.

The Hawks have called
PHILIPS ARENA
home since 1999.

32

The talented big man filled the team's most glaring hole. "Championship teams start from the inside out," noted Wilkens. "We need a stronger presence down low in order to contend." The 7-foot-2 Mutombo had averaged nearly four blocked shots a game in five years with Denver. "He's an intimidator," said forward Alan Henderson, who joined Atlanta around the same time and provided rebounding and scoring punch. "Now he's *our* intimidator." Mutombo was named NBA Defensive Player of the Year in his first two seasons with the team. But neither Wilkens nor Mutombo could solve Atlanta's ongoing problem. The Hawks got to the playoffs almost every year. But they never lasted long enough to contend for another NBA title.

The Hawks lost in the conference semifinals after the strike-shortened 1998–99 season. They moved to the newly constructed Philips Arena for the following season. The team went 21–20 in its new nest. However, the Hawks managed just 7 wins on the road. That resulted in the team's worst-ever record (28–54). Speedy guard Jason Terry made the NBA All-Rookie second team and "Mount Mutombo" led the NBA in rebounding. That season marked the start of an eight-year playoff drought.

Russian center **ALEXANDER VOLKOV** played in Atlanta for two seasons.

34

WORLD TRAVELERS

ATLANTA VS. RUSSIAN ALL-STAR TEAM, JULY 1988

Political tensions between the U.S. and Russia were high as Atlanta became the first NBA team to play in Russia. The Hawks endured horrible food during the 15-day tour. "Cucumbers and tomatoes," moaned one player. "The milk had lumps in it." Atlanta won two of the three games. The series helped Eastern European players gain entrance to the NBA. That had never happened before. One of the first was Alexander Volkov, who joined Atlanta the following year. "I was the happiest guy in the world that moment when I put on a Hawks uniform and put my shoes on the floor for the first game. It was a dream come true."

LEGENDS OF THE HARDWOOD

T he team never won more than 35 games during this stretch. The low point came in 2004–05. Atlanta won just 13 games. It was the worst record in the NBA that season. The team's winning percentage of .159 was its lowest ever. The one consolation was that Atlanta's young players got lots of playing time. Explosive forward Marvin Williams joined the team the following year. He expressed the determination of his teammates by saying, "I want to win. We're all going to work hard. We're going to be young, but at least we're going to learn the game of basketball from the coaches."

BACK FROM THE DEPTHS

That positive attitude paid off. The Hawks improved to 26–56 and then 30–52. Their 37–45 mark in 2007–08 was good enough to return to the playoffs. They pushed the top-seeded and highly

Forward **MARVIN WILLIAMS** helped the Hawks return to the playoffs.

JOE JOHNSON led the Hawks in points, assists, and three-pointers in 2005–06.

> "OUR DEFENSE IS THE ONE CONSTANT, THE ONE THING WE'VE BEEN ABLE TO COUNT ON EVERY NIGHT SO FAR," SAID WOODSON. "IT'S NOT ALWAYS THE PRETTIEST THING TO THE CASUAL EYE, BUT IT'S WHAT WINS IN OUR LEAGUE."

favored Celtics to seven games in the first round before bowing out. This performance generated new respect for the Hawks. A key figure in the resurgence was shooting guard/small forward Joe Johnson. He joined the team in 2005. Eventually, he became a six-time All-Star. Another was rookie power forward/center Al Horford, a triple-threat down low who could score, block shots, and pull down rebounds.

39

Atlanta won 47 games in 2008–09. The team was becoming increasingly confident with coach Mike Woodson's emphasis on playing solid, smothering defense. "Our defense is the one constant, the one thing we've been able to count on every night so far," said Woodson. "It's not always the prettiest thing to the casual eye, but it's what wins in our league." Atlanta won the first round of the playoffs before falling to Cleveland in the next round.

40

CARRYING THE ROCK

KYLE KORVER, SHOOTING GUARD/SMALL FORWARD, 6-FOOT-7, 2012–17

Kyle Korver set a record of 127 games of making at least one 3-point shot from 2012 to 2014. He practiced his long-range shooting every day, using a 20-point checklist. He also practiced misogi. This is a Japanese purification ritual that usually involves some form of intense physical activity. Before Korver's first mosigi, he paddleboarded across 25 miles (40.2 km) of open ocean. At first, he was bleeding and miserable. "But eventually, you hit a point where we're not going to turn around. We're not going to stop," he said. Another misogi was carrying an 85-pound (38.6 kg) rock underwater. "Everything falls into place by doing the smallest thing perfectly," Korver explained. "That lesson from the misogi carried over to my shooting."

Versatile center **AL HORFORD** earned All-Star honors four times.

he 2009–10 season was even better. The Hawks won 53 games, the first time they had reached the 50-win plateau since 1997–98. "It's been a good season," said Horford. He had emerged as one of the NBA's top rebounders, averaging more than nine boards per game. "But there's more to the team than just this." Then Atlanta fell back a pace, losing in the conference semifinals for the second straight year. The two seasons after that resulted in further playoff losses.

The 2012–13 season concluded with Atlanta's sixth straight playoff appearance following the eight-year drought. But the team still couldn't

Forward **KYLE KORVER** added a consistent spark to Atlanta's outside offense.

42

Head coach **MIKE BUDENHOLZER** talks to **DENNIS SCHRODER** during a game against the Denver Nuggets.

break through. Team officials hired new coach Mike Budenholzer. As a longtime San Antonio Spurs assistant, Budenholzer learned a lot. He emphasized selflessness and putting the team first. Hawks three-point shooting star Kyle Korver played for three teams before coming to Atlanta. He said, "I feel like every coach is either really good at X's and O's or a really good personality manager, and there aren't many coaches who know how to walk the middle. Bud? I've never seen a coach at any level who does it better than him."

Speedy guard **JEFF TEAGUE** was a leader in dishing out assists to teammates.

"I FEEL LIKE EVERY COACH IS EITHER
REALLY GOOD AT X'S AND O'S OR A
REALLY GOOD PERSONALITY MANAGER,
AND THERE AREN'T MANY COACHES WHO
KNOW HOW TO WALK THE MIDDLE."

"Bud" wasn't an overnight success. The Hawks had their first losing record in six years, but they still returned to the playoffs. However, they fell to the Indiana Pacers four games to three in the first round. Little about that season prepared Atlanta fans for the 2014–15 season. After starting 7–6, the Hawks were almost unstoppable for more than two months. They ran away with the Eastern Conference's Southeast Division championship. They finished with a franchise-best 60–22 mark. The Hawks advanced to the conference finals but lost in four games. One factor in the team's success was point guard Jeff Teague. His outstanding play led to his first NBA All-Star selection in 2015. Another key cog was power forward Paul Millsap. He led the team in scoring and rebounding. Though the Hawks fell back to 48 wins in 2015–16, they easily made the playoffs. They beat the Celtics in the first round. But Cleveland swept Atlanta in the next round. Before the 2016–17 season, center Dwight Howard joined his hometown team. The Hawks won 43 games but fell to Washington in the first round of the playoffs.

As of 2017, it had been 59 years since Bob Pettit led the Hawks to their one and only NBA title. Only the Sacramento Kings had gone longer without winning the championship. Buoyed by what Budenholzer accomplished, Hawks fans felt confident. They hoped that another championship banner would soon hang in Philips Arena.

SELECTED BIBLIOGRAPHY

Ballard, Chris. *The Art of a Beautiful Game: The Thinking Fan's Tour of the NBA*. New York: Simon & Schuster, 2010.

Bleacher Report. "Atlanta Hawks." http://bleacherreport.com/atlanta -hawks.

Hubbard, Jan, ed. *The Official NBA Basketball Encyclopedia*. 3rd edition. New York: Doubleday, 2000.

NBA.com. "Atlanta Hawks." http://www.nba.com/hawks/.

Sports Illustrated. *Sports Illustrated Basketball's Greatest*. New York: Sports Illustrated, 2014.

WEBSITES

DUCKSTERS BASKETBALL: NBA

http://www.ducksters.com/sports/national_basketball_association.php

Learn more about NBA history, rules, positions, strategy, drills, and other topics.

JR. NBA

http://jr.nba.com/

This kids site has games, videos, game results, team and player information, statistics, and more.

Note: Every effort has been made to ensure that any websites listed above were active at the time of publication. However, because of the nature of the Internet, it is impossible to guarantee that these sites will remain active indefinitely or that their contents will not be altered.

INDEX